W9-AMP-297

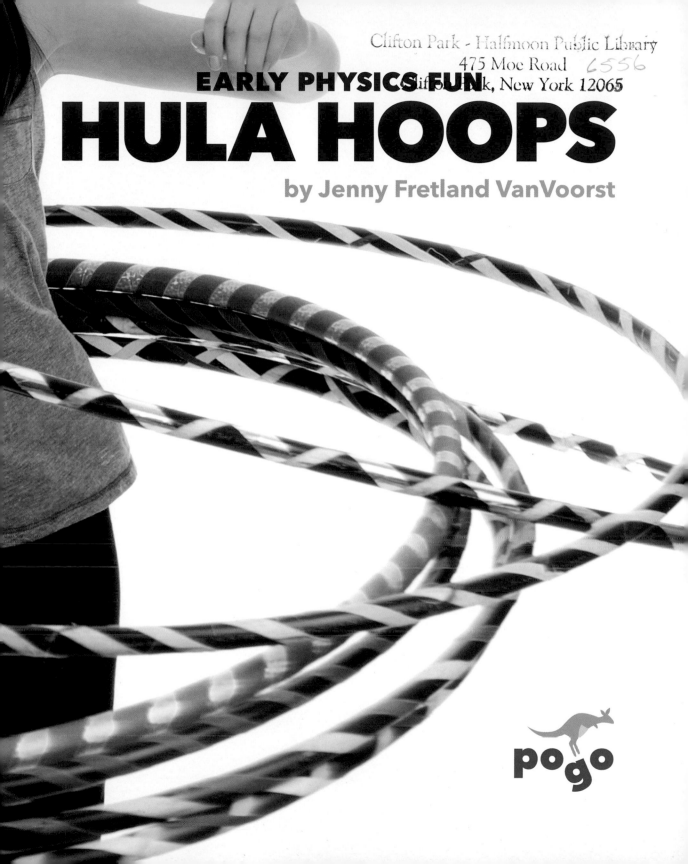

EARLY PHYSICS FUN

HULA HOOPS

by Jenny Fretland VanVoorst

pogo

Ideas for Parents and Teachers

Pogo Books let children practice reading informational text while introducing them to nonfiction features such as headings, labels, sidebars, maps, and diagrams, as well as a table of contents, glossary, and index.

Carefully leveled text with a strong photo match offers early fluent readers the support they need to succeed.

Before Reading

- "Walk" through the book and point out the various nonfiction features. Ask the student what purpose each feature serves.
- Look at the glossary together. Read and discuss the words.

Read the Book

- Have the child read the book independently.
- Invite him or her to list questions that arise from reading.

After Reading

- Discuss the child's questions. Talk about how he or she might find answers to those questions.
- Prompt the child to think more. Ask: Have you ever played with a hula hoop? How long could you keep it spinning?

Pogo Books are published by Jump!
5357 Penn Avenue South
Minneapolis, MN 55419
www.jumplibrary.com

Library of Congress Cataloging-in-Publication Data

Names: Fretland VanVoorst, Jenny, 1972- author.
Title: Hula hoops / by Jenny Fretland VanVoorst.
Description: Minneapolis, MN : Jump!, Inc. [2016] |
Series: Early physics fun | Audience: Ages 7-10. |
Includes bibliographical references and index.
Identifiers: LCCN 2015045035 |
ISBN 9781620313169 (hardcover: alk. paper)
Subjects: LCSH: Torque–Juvenile literature. |
Friction–Juvenile literature. | Force and energy–
Juvenile literature. | Physics–Study and teaching–
Juvenile literature.
Classification: LCC QC73.4.F744 2016 |
DDC 531.34–dc23
LC record available at http://lccn.loc.gov/2015045035

Series Designer: Anna Peterson
Photo Researcher: Anna Peterson

Photo Credits: Alamy, 10-11; Fotosearch, 4; Getty, 6-7, 8-9, 13, 20-21; iStock, 16-17; Shutterstock, cover, 1, 5, 23; SuperStock, 12; Thinkstock, 3, 18-19.

Printed in the United States of America at Corporate Graphics in North Mankato, Minnesota.

TABLE OF CONTENTS

CHAPTER 1

TORQUE

Have you ever spun a hula hoop around your waist? Could you keep it going? Or did it fall down right away?

Hula hoops spin or fall based on the **laws** of **physics**. Physics is the science that explores matter and how it moves.

When you spin a hula hoop, your body is the source of the hoop's movement. You power its spin by moving your waist and hips.

When you wiggle your body to move the hoop, you're applying **torque**. Torque is a twisting **force**. It causes the hoop to spin.

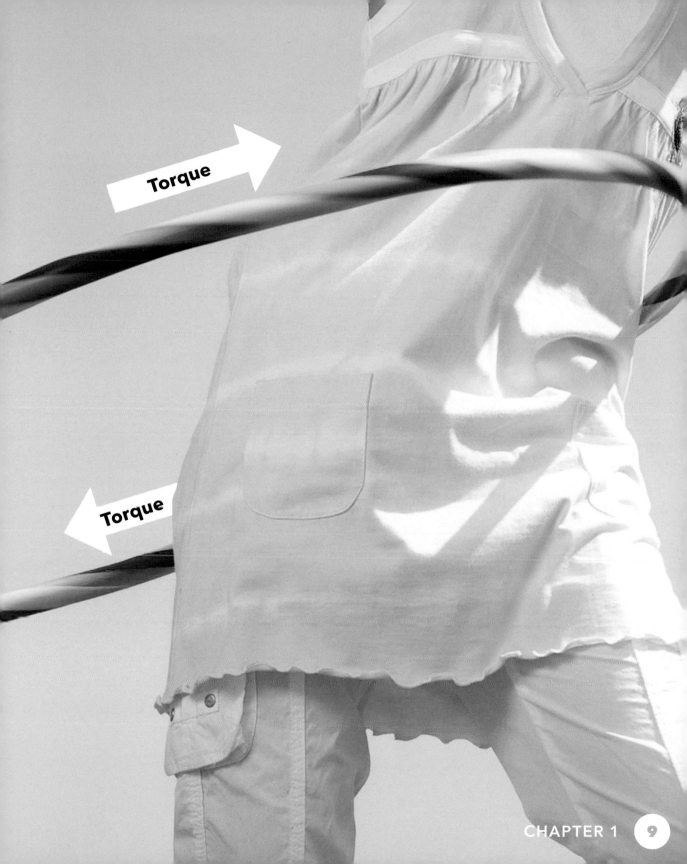

Torque

Torque

The torque needed depends on weight and size of the hoop. A large or heavy hoop is harder to keep up. It spins more slowly. This means it needs more torque. A smaller or lighter hoop needs less.

DID YOU KNOW?

You can spin a hoop around any part of your body. Different sized rings work better for different parts of the body.

CHAPTER 2

NEWTON'S FIRST LAW

Newton's First Law of Motion is one of the most important laws of physics. It says that an object continues to move or rest unless acted upon by an outside force. So what does this have to do with hula hoops?

It means that a spinning hoop will spin until another force stops it. That can be your hand grabbing the hoop.

It can also be **gravity**. Gravity is the constant force that pulls anything with **mass** back toward the earth. Gravity is always working against the hoop.

Gravity

When you spin a hula hoop, gravity slows the spin. It makes the hoop drop to the ground.

But by moving your hips, you keep the hoop moving. This helps the hoop resist gravity.

CHAPTER 3

....

FRICTION

Friction is a force that works both for and against the hula hoop.

It occurs whenever two objects rub against each other. It causes them to resist each other.

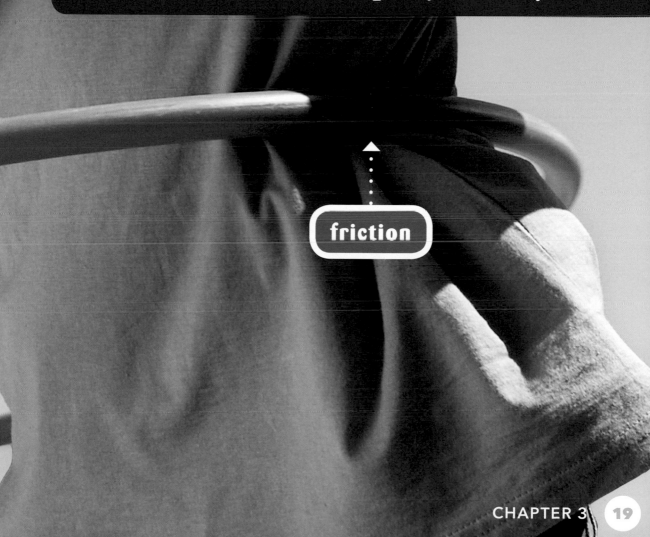

When the hoop spins, it rubs against your clothing. The rubbing slows the spin. It gives gravity a chance.

But friction also works against gravity. How? It "sticks" the hoop to your body.

friction

This mix of physics forces makes hula hooping both challenging and fun. So grab a hoop and give it a spin. It's science!

How does friction slow a hoop's spin? It turns motion into heat. There's not enough to feel. But it's there.

Try rubbing your hands together. Now can you feel the heat? That's friction!

ACTIVITIES & TOOLS

HULA HOOP SPIN TEST

Let's see how the size and weight of a hula hoop affects how long you can keep it spinning. You will need access to a variety of hula hoops of differing weights and diameters.

❶ First try a light hula hoop with a large diameter. Record how long you can keep it spinning.

❷ Now try spinning a hoop of the same diameter that is heavier. Record your results.

❸ Now try a smaller, lighter hoop. How does this one compare to the previous two?

❹ How about a smaller, heavier hoop?

❺ Compare the results. Which combination allowed you to spin the hoop the longest? Which combination made spinning the hoop the most difficult?

GLOSSARY

force: An influence (as a push or pull) that tends to produce a change in the speed or direction of motion of something.

friction: The force that resists motion between bodies in contact.

gravity: The attraction of the earth for bodies at or near its surface.

law: A basic rule or principle.

mass: The amount of matter in a body; it differs from weight in that weight is a measurement of the force of gravity on a mass.

Newton's First Law of Motion: The physics law that states that unless acted upon by an outside force, an object in motion tends to stay in motion at the same speed and direction.

physics: The science that involves the study of matter and how it moves through space and time; it includes concepts such as energy and force.

rhythm gymnastics: A sport in which athletes combine gymnastics moves with artistic use of clubs, hoops, balls, ribbons, or ropes.

torque: A twisting force that tends to cause rotation.

INDEX

TO LEARN MORE

Learning more is as easy as 1, 2, 3.

1) Go to www.factsurfer.com

2) Enter "hulahoops" into the search box.

3) Click the "Surf" button to see a list of websites.

With factsurfer, finding more information is just a click away.